My Journey's End

Dennis J. Billy, C.Ss.R.

En Route Books and Media, LLC
Saint Louis, MO

✺ENROUTE
Make the time

En Route Books and Media, LLC
5705 Rhodes Avenue
St. Louis, MO 63109

Contact us at
contactus@enroutebooksandmedia.com

Cover Credit: Sebastian Mahfood

Copyright 2026 Dennis J. Billy, C.Ss.R.

ISBN-13: 979-8-88870-497-4
Library of Congress Control Number:
Available online at https://catalog.loc.gov

All rights reserved. No part of this book may be reproduced, stored in a retrieval system, or transmitted in any form, or by any means, electronic, mechanical, photocopying, or otherwise, without the prior written permission of the author.

For my fellow travelers

Not all those who wander are lost.
J.R.R. Tolkien

Table of Contents

Again 1
And Talk 2
At the Very Least 3
Beside Me 4
By Me 5
Challenges 6
Discovered 7
For Them 8
Friends 9
From Light to Light 10
Happens 11
Hungry Hearts 12
I Have Looked 13
In Its Shadow 14
Into the Wild! 15
It Doesn't Matter 16
Laughter 17
Left Behind 18
Listen 19
Look Beyond 20
More Pressing Concerns 21
My Journey's End 22
My Own Choosing 23

My Path 24

Never Before 25

On Life! 26

One Step 27

Or Hoped For 28

Or Not 29

Promises 30

Rest 31

Seeking 32

Still to Come 33

The Morning Light 34

The New Year 35

The Next Step 36

The Present Moment 37

The Same 38

There is an Aching 39

To Decide 40

Whatever Lies Ahead 41

When My Loneliness 42

With Open Eyes 43

Within 44

Without Bounds 45

A Deeper Light 46

About Myself 47

Ahead 48

And We Rise!	49
And Yet Another	50
At a Moment	51
By His Side	52
Friendship	53
From Whom It Comes	54
Home	55
I Look	56
I Open	57
In Days to Come	58
In the Midst	59
Taking Me	60
Letting Go	61
Like Breathing	62
Limitless	63
Look Around You	64
My Journey	65
My Longing Heart	66
Resurrection	67
Seen	68
So Very Different	69
Staying the Course	70
Takes Us	71
There Was	72
This Innocent Child	73

To Our Hearts 75
Together 76
What I See 77
With Gratitude 78
With His 79
Your Answer? 80

Again

People come

And go

In and out

Of our lives.

Still, there are

Some who remain.

Be grateful

For those

Who stay

And pray

For those

Who leave.

Let us live

In the hope

That one day

We will all

See each other

Again.

And Talk

I think about myself
And where I've come from.
I also think of you
And where you've come from.
From what I can tell,
You and I come from
 The same Source,
The same Place,
The same Person,
The same Dream.
Shouldn't that make us
Brothers and sisters,
Members of our
One human family?
If not, let us
Sit down together,
See where we stand,
Silence ourselves,
Look each other
In the eye,
And talk.

At the Very Least

I am born
Into a family
Unknown to me.
I know not how
I will be raised.
I have no idea
Whatsoever
Of how I will
Be shaped,
Educated,
Or formed.
My only hope
Is to listen
To that still
Small voice
Deep within me
That will,
At the very least,
Point out the way
I should walk
And encourage me
To embrace it.

Beside Me

I do not wish
To walk
This path alone.
Yet I do,
Day in
And Day out.
Hoping that
One Day
Someone
Will choose
To walk
Beside me.

By Me

I am lonely
At this moment,
As we all are,
From time
To time,
Especially when
We face our
Final moments
And ponder
What is to come,
Beyond what
The present
Allows us to see.
At such times
I think of all
The lives who
Have touched me
And all whom
I have touched,
Past, present,
And future.
I remember
All that has passed,
And look to my end
With love
And deepfelt gratitude
For all the lives
I have touched
And who have been touched,
If ever so slightly
By me.

Challenges

I open my eyes
And awake from sleep.
A new day reveals
Itself to me.
I ponder
What lies ahead,
Take a deep breath,
And face
The challenges ahead.

Discovered

I go inside
myself
To discover
Who I am.
In doing so,
I come to see
That I
Have already
Been discovered!

For Them

Happiness
Does not depend
On what you feel,
Or even on
How you think.
It comes from
Something
Deep inside,
Something
Only a few
Of us sense
And follow
Through on.
It comes from
Walking behind
Those we have
Been called
To serve
And looking out
For them,
One day
At a time.

Friends

I have had friends,
In the morning
And the evening
Of my Life.
Some have
Stuck by me,
Through thick
And thin,
Others have simply
Faded away
Into the past,
Never to be seen
Again.
What kind
Of friend
Are you
To me
Or am I
To you?
These are
Questions
To reflect upon
And answer
In the deepest recesses
Of our hearts.

From Light to Light

I walk
In the Woods
On a dark,
Lonely Night.
I know not
Where it leads,
And am anxious
For Myself,
My Life,
My Present,
My Past,
My Future,
My very Being.
Step by step
I walk
An unknown Path.
Step by step
I trod
A muddy Road.
Step by step
I walk Inside
Without,
And Outside
Within.
Step by step
I encounter
An unknown Part
Of Myself,
A missing Part,
Inside of Myself
And Without.
Step by step
I discover
A Darkness
Within Me
That leads
From Darkness
To Darkness,
From Shadow
To Shadow,
From Dawn
To Dawn,
From Sleep
To Sleep,
From Morning
To Morning—
From Light
To Light.

Happens

Whatever happens,
Happens!
How we react
To what has happened
Reveals to us
What has
Happened.

Hungry Hearts

I have traveled
Miles upon miles,
Roads upon roads,
Seas upon seas,
Lands upon lands,
And everywhere
I have gone
I have found
Nothing but
Hungry hearts.

I Have Looked

I have looked
For the meaning
Of Life.
I have looked
To the past,
The present,
And the future,
And still
Have no bearings,
No direction,
As to where
I should go.
I am wandering
Without direction.
I only ask
That someone,
Sometime,
Would lead me
Home.

In Its Shadow

I fall Asleep
And Dream
Of Things
Beyond
My Imagination.
I enter into Them
And Feel
As Though
They are Real.
I Wake Up
And Come
To my Senses.
But that Dream,
To this Day,
Lingers
In my Mind
And Heart,
And I Live
Forever
In Its Shadow.

Into the Wild!

I walk a lonely path
And contemplate
The mountains and trees,
Brooks and paths,
Rivers and streams
The inner and outer
Sense of self
To no end.
I breathe in
The surroundings,
The leaves
And trees,
The rivers
And fords,
The depths
Highlands
And lowlands.
All this I receive
Into myself
And release
My failures,
Frustrations,
Anxieties,
Disappointments,
Ups and downs,
One by one—
Into the wild!

It Doesn't Matter

It doesn't matter
How long you have lived,
Whether you have
Been snatched
From your mother's womb,
Or breathed your last
At a ripe old age.
What matters
Is how you
Have lived your Life.
What matters is
How you have spent
The Time given you.
What matters
Is how you live
This day,
And every day,
And all days following—
In the Here and Now.

Laughter

It's okay
To be silly
From time
To time.
Let's not
Take things
Too seriously.
Let's laugh.
Let's savor
The moment
And be grateful
For what we have.

Left Behind

I awake
Each day
And think of
What lay
Before me.
I live
My life,
One day
At a time,
And wonder,
At times,
From moment
To moment,
Day to day,
If whatever
Lay before me
I might have
Somehow
Indiscernibly,
Unknowingly
And without regret,
Left behind.

Listen

Listen to your heart
And follow its lead.
Be aware, however,
That what you may
Think your heart
Is telling you is true,
May or may not be so.
Listen to your heart.
Delve deep within.
Listen to that
Still small voice
Within you
That guides
And nourishes you.
Listen to it.

Reflect.
Think.
Discern.
Pray.
Share your thoughts
With someone you trust.
Decide.
Act.
Follow through.
And don't ever,
Ever,
Turn you head
And look back.

Look Beyond

Look beyond
What you see.
Look with your
Inner eyes.
Ponder
What appears
Before you.
Reflect on what
You ponder.
Act on what
You reflect upon.
Become what
You act.
Act on what
You have
Become.

More Pressing Concerns

The Past cannot be changed,
And we should not dwell on it.
The Future is yet to unfold
And is doing so at this very moment.
We should allow it to happen,
Yet not be anxious about its outcome.
There are other, more pressing concerns.

My Journey's End

There are times
When I feel lost.
There are other times
When I have found
My bearings
And can continue
My walk.
Most times,
I waver between
The two
And simply hope
That I will reach,
Wherever I am going,
By placing one foot
Before the other,
Step by step,
Until I reach
My journey's end.

My Own Choosing

I travel a road
And know not
Where it leads.
I follow that path
And realize
It is not
The way
I should walk.
I turn back,
Difficult as
It may seem,
And travel
A different road,
That will
Lead me,
In Time,
And Space
To a Place
Unknown,
But of my
Own choosing.

My Path

A path lies before me,
And I take it not knowing
Where it will lead.
I walk this way,
Wherever it goes
Because it is my path,
Chosen especially for me,
The one given me,
And no one else,
From all Eternity.
This path I must follow
To discover myself and
The role I am asked to play
In the unfolding of
The mysterious ways
Of what the future
Unfolds in my life
And those of others.

Never Before

I close my eyes,
Fall asleep,
And dream
Of things
Unimaginable.
I open my eyes
To the rising sun
And see
Things
Never before
Imagined.

On Life!

Do not live
In the virtual world.
Live in the real world!
If you don't,
You will virtually
Be missing out
On Life!

One Step

One step
At a time,
Day by day,
Here and now,
Now and always!
Wherever
I find myself,
I will always
Seek to help
The helpless
And those
In need.

Or Hoped For

I open my eyes
And see what
Appears before me.
I close my eyes,
Open my heart,
See my Inner Self,
And ponder things
Beyond all telling,
Beyond what
I could ever
Have thought of,
Or imagined,
Beyond whatever
I could ever have
Dreamed of
Or hoped for.

Or Not

I open my Eyes
And see what
I cannot See,
Sense what
I cannot Dream.
Imagine what
I cannot Imagine:
Life before Birth,
Death before Life,
Being before Self,
Over and Out,
Within and Without,
Before and After,
This Way and That,
Every which Way
You can Go—-
Or Not.

Promises

We expect
What is
To come
In light
Of what
We have
Experienced.
Still,
We need
To be open
To what
The future
Tells us
Of the past
And what
It promises.

Rest

I Walk
In Darkness
And am Wary
Of my Steps.
I know Not.
What Each
Will Bring.
I Lose
The Path
Before Me
And Forget
Myself
In the Hope
Of One Day
Finding Myself
At Peace
And at Rest.

Seeking

Life comes
And goes,
As they say.
I find myself
Wondering
If my Life
Is Coming
Or Going,
Headed
Elsewhere,
Or Seeking
Its ultimate
Source.

Still to Come

I try to live
In the present,
But the past
Haunts me
To this very day.
I seek forgiveness
For what I have done
And not done.
I live in hope,
Each and
Every day,
Of my Life,
And seek
That one day
I might become
The person
I am called to be—-
And still to become.

The Morning Light

The sun goes down,
As darkness descends
And heralds the night,
As sleep overtakes me,
And I close my eyes
To consciousness,
I find myself
Floating in a sea
Of wild dreams
And visions,
As I lose myself
In a subliminal world
That enters my mind
And helps me
To sort out my past,
Decipher it,
Make peace with it,
And open my eyes
To the morning light.

The New Year

As a New Year Begins,
I look upon my Past
And peer into my Future.
I hope that what I have
Learned
Will influence my next Steps.
Otherwise, I am Doomed
To repeat my past Mistakes.
May this New Year open my
Eyes
To Future Possibilities
That will influence my
Choices
And Future Actions.
May the Coming Year
Be a Harbinger of Change,
Within and Without—
Of Good Things
To Come.

The Next Step

I Travel
Into Darkness,
Yet know Not
Where my Journey
Will End.
I Hope this
Darkness
Will Lead
To Light,
And Light
To Dawn,
And Dawn
To Dusk.
I Travel
Into an Unknown,
Into a Realm
Of Uncertainty,
Where Doubts,
Haunt me
Inhabit me,
Challenge me
And Take me,
All of Me—
To the Next Step.

The Present Moment

I'd like
To walk
Through Life
One moment,
One second,
One minute,
One hour,
One day
At a time. I
If only
It would be
So easy.
Living in the
Present Moment
Is the work
Of a Lifetime.

The Same

When I opened
my eyes to Life,
I always relied
On the help
Of others.
As I live my Life
This day,
I will always seek
To do the same.

There is an Aching

There is an aching
Inside me.
I know not from
Where it comes.
It is a deep
Yearning,
Inexplicable
Groaning,
A sense of
Both Loss
And Gain.
I experience
This longing
At odd times,
During the Day,
At Night,
And even
In my Dreams.
My hope is that
These yearnings,
Taken together,
Will lead me,
Day by day,
Step by step,
Moment by moment,
To my journey's
End.

To Decide

Life ebbs
And flows
It comes,
And goes.
We, who are
Immersed in Life,
Must make
A radical choice.
Am I to move
With the flow,
Or swim against
The current?
That choice
Is for you
To decide.

Whatever Lies Ahead

My journey through Life
Has certainly had
Its share of ups and downs.
The question is not
How to avoid them
But how to navigate them.
Life is full of the unforeseen.
Let us embrace Life
As well as the unknown.
Let us not try to avoid them,
But embrace them,
Navigate them
Treasure them,
Savor them,
Until they one day merge
And reveal to us
A clear path that leads us
To the destiny,
That awaits us
At the end of our journey—-
And whatever lies ahead.

When My Loneliness

I am secluded
In a lonely spot.
I linger there,
Awhile,
And breathe in
The Beauty
Of the moment.
I take a deep breath,
Ponder the world
Around me,
Let out
A deep,
Lonely sigh,
And yearn
For the day
When my Loneliness
Will turn to Bliss.

With Open Eyes

I close my eyes
At the end
Of a busy day
And look forward
To the dreams
That are to come.
Often they are not
What I expected,
Or ignored,
Or even wanted.
To live Life
One must expect,
The unexpected,
See the unseen,
Hear the unheard,
Live in uncertainty,
And walk into the future—-
With open eyes.

Within

I travel to
And fro,
Here
And there,
Near
And far,
And sincerely
Wonder
If the real
Traveling
Is really that
Which you
And I
Start,
Here
And there,
Near
And far,
From Within.

Without Bounds

Like a little child
I open my heart
To those who
Care for me.
I look to them
For how to care
For myself
And others.
I smile when
My care for others
Is reciprocated.
When it is not,
I continue to love
Without bounds.

A Deeper Light

Darkness surrounds me,
Yet Light pierces through
My unconscious projections.
I struggle against
The Darkness,
And find myself unable
To live as I ought.
I wander in pain
And feel completely lost
In the Darkness within me.
Still, Light does not forsake me.
It illumines my soul,
Gives me peace,
Comforts me,
And casts out whatever
Darkness lies
Within my soul,
As it travels
Within me
Into a Deeper Light.

About Myself

I think about myself
And wonder who I am.
I ponder that enigma
And face an
Existential choice,
One deep
Within my heart,
One that I
Have struggled with,
Time and again.
Am I the center
Of my universe,
Or not?
Do I decide
What is
Right and wrong
Or not?
Do I live
My life
According to
My own whims
And passions?
Or not?
What else
Can I choose?
Where else
Can I turn?
To whom
Shall I go?
What I decide,
In pondering
This question,
Will have
Repercussions
Throughout my Life
And the lives
Of many others.
I need help
In all this!
In dire moments,
These deep
And darkest moments,
I turn to You,
My Lord.
Help me to decide
The way I should walk.
Help me
To walk this way
Deliberately,
Prudently,
And Wisely.

Ahead

I wonder
What lies
Beyond
The pale
Of Death.
I know
What I have
Been told
To believe,
And indeed
I do!
Still, I wonder
What lies
Beyond.
I await
Its coming
And look
Forward
To experiencing
Whatever it
May be
That lies
Ahead.

And We Rise!

Some people say
We are born,
We live,
And we die.
Others say
We are born,
We live,
And we Rise!

And Yet Another

I listen
And am
Listened to.
Silence forms
Strong bonds,
From one
To another,
From another
To another,
And to another,
And yet Another
Unspoken Friend.

At a Moment

I am at a moment
Of change
In my Life.
I always
Find change
Difficult
To navigate.
I know not
What to expect.
I wonder if
I will fit in,
Be acknowledged,
Accepted,
Lauded,
Looked down on,
Or possibly abused.
I tend to dwell
In the past
And wonder
If I could ever
Recreate it.

Yet, that is not
Where I am
Called to be.
I must not dwell
In the past,
Nor define myself
By future hopes.
I must live
In the present
And seek the Lord
This day,
Every day,
Wherever I am,
And happen to be,
Here or there,
Near or far,
In the people
I meet.

By His Side

I am grateful for Life,
For each and every moment,
For each and every breath!
I am grateful for all
That has happened,
And for all still to come.
I am grateful for
Whatever happens!
I say this because,
Whether in
Good Times
Or in Bad
Whether in Trial
Or in Pain,
Whether in this Time
Or the Next,
The Lord
Our God
Accompanies us
On our Journey,
And with Him
We have nothing
To fear.
The Good Lord
Leads me
To where
I need to be—
Close by His side.

Friendship

I look upon my past
And see so many things.
I have done wrong
And in so many ways!
I feel lost in my
Guilt, and still do.
What can I do?
How can I
Ease the pain?
How can I overcome
The pain of my past?

Rest, my friend.
Let go of your
Present concerns.
Be silent…
Rest in my silence.
Whatever your hurt,
Whatever your wound,
Whatever your longing,
Know that God loves
And forgives you
And welcomes you
Into His most intimate
Friendship.

From Whom It Comes

I am who I am,
Yet also whom
I am called
To be.
I struggle
To become
My better self,
Yet understand
That to do so,
I must relinquish
My will
To the One
From Whom
It comes.

Home

What I do
And not do
Shapes me
And haunts me.
I am a product
Of my actions
But also
Of my omissions.
I look back
On my past,
And have
So many regrets.
My only hope is
Is that
The Good Lord
Will look down
On me,
Smile on me,
Extend His hand
To me
And one day,
Over time,
Embrace me
And welcome me
Home.

I Look

My life lies
Before me.
I look back
And wonder
If my past
Will haunt me.
I look deep
Within myself
And hear
A voice saying,
"Do not be afraid.
I know your past,
Your present,
And your future.
Trust me.
Place your hands
In my hands.
I promise
To lead you home."

I Open

I open my eyes
And face
The challenges
Of the new day.
I open my heart
And ask the Lord
To help me
Do what
I must do.

In Days to Come

I look back on my Life
And have so much
To be grateful for:
My mother and father,
My brothers and sister,
My cousins,
My extended family,
My teachers,
My coaches,
My friends.
I am grateful
For all who have
Journeyed with me
On this exciting,
Yet dangerous,
Adventure
Called Life.

I am grateful
For so many things,
For all that
Has been,
Is present,
And still to come.
I am grateful
For the Lord's
Presence
In my Life.
And I am
Eternally Grateful
For where
He will
Lead me—
In days to come.

In the Midst

In the midst
Of Darkness,
My senses
Are both
Numbed
And silenced.
I wander about
Not knowing
Where I am headed.
I seek to open up
My broken
Wearied Life,
And surrender it
Here and now,
Now and always,
Forever and ever,
Into Your Inscrutable,
Unfathomable Light.

Taking Me

I walk a path of my own making,
Yet seek within my heart
The direction I must take.
I listen to that still small voice
Inside my wounded heart,
And listen as best I can
To where it is taking me.
I seek to follow it
And follow to seek it.
I journey with this voice
Within me and ponder
With all my heart
The direction it
Is taking me.

Letting Go

I let go of my dreams
And seek to follow
The voice within me.
I have no idea
Where it will lead me.
I can only trust
That the voice
I trust will lead me,
Albeit through
Winding ways,
To my journey
Home.

Like Breathing

Prayer is like breathing.
It's hard to get through
The day on a single breath.
We need to breathe in and out
Over and over again,
So much so that we don't
Even think about it.
In the same way,
We cannot get through
A single day, let alone
An entire Life, without
Talking to God
And Listening to Him
Deep within the depths
Of our broken,
Yearning hearts.

Limitless

There is a Limit to Life:
Birth and Death.
The question is
Whether that Limit
Is Limited,
Or Limitless.

Look Around You

Look around you
And see what
You can see.
Everything there,
Wherever you turn,
Comes from the hand
Of a generous Giver.
Should we not,
Day in and day out,
Try our best,
In some way,
To reciprocate?

My Journey

I look back
On my life,
And have so
Many regrets.
I am ashamed
Of many things
I have done—
And their memories
Still haunt me.
I know I am not worthy
Of God's love for me,
But I also believe
That God's love for me
Is not limited
To my weak,
Impoverished self.

I trust in the Lord.
I believe.
I seek to love
As Jesus loves.
I know I have
A long way to go,
But that is what
I hope for.
I place my hope
In Him,
And in Him alone—
As I continue
My journey.

My Longing Heart

I listen to the silence
Deep within my heart
And dance to the
Soft, gentle music
That strums my soul.
Such silence
Touches me,
Moves me,
Warms me,
Cleanses me
Quiets me,
And Conforms me,
Day after day,
Night after night,
To the lonely movement
That strums the strings
Of my ever searching
Longing heart.

Resurrection

Am I a disembodied spirit,
Or an enfleshed soul?
Is my body an intimate
Part of my human identity,
Or just an accidental feature
That I can do with as I wish?
These questions are not new.
Christians have struggled
With them for millennia.
We have always opted for embodiment,
And will continue to do so
Until the resurrection of the dead!

Seen

Enjoy Life!
Such is
God's will
For you!
Only remember
That what
He wills
Cannot always
Be clearly
Seen.

So Very Different

I look at myself
And see
What I see.
I look at myself
Through the eyes
Of Christ
And see
Something different,
Oh, so very
Different!

Staying the Course

I walk alone,
Yet not alone,
For, with every
Step I take,
Someone
Has always
Been behind me,
To catch me
When I fall,
Comfort me
When I am sad,
Heal me
Of my wounds,
And gently
Help me
Get back
On my feet,
Stay the course,
And lead me home.

Takes Us

We gather in Life
But ultimately
Must let go
Of all we have.
Life is all about
Letting go.
The longer
We hold on
To what
We possess
And all that
Has taken
Possession
Of our souls,
The harder
Will it be
For us
To spread
Our wings
And fly
To where
The wind,
And the Power
Behind it,
Seeks to
Take us.

There Was

There was a time
When I was not
Conscious of myself.
I lived from
Moment to moment,
And had no sense
Of who I was
Or where
I came from.
Then, one day,
Something happened.
Words fall short.
I cannot explain.
It was as if a Light
Had been turned on
Within my soul.
And I could see things
About myself
That I had never
Seen before.

I saw myself
As I truly was,
And I recognized
Someone,
Another,
A Long-Lost Friend,
A Bereaved Loss,
A Distant Parent,
And in my Loss
I could see
My Creator,
For whom He was.
And from that
Moment on
My Life
Has never been
The same

This Innocent Child

This innocent child,
Born in the Dark of Night,
Lying in a manger,
Wrapped in swaddling
 clothes,
Kept warm by ox and lamb,
Suckled at his mother's
 breasts,
Heralded by Angels,
Reverenced by Shepherds,
Honored by Wise Men
In the Still of Night,
This Innocent Child
Harkens the Dawn
Of a New Day,
A Day for which
The World has
Forever waited,
Hoped for,
Longed for,
Yearned for…
And the time has Come!
Yes, the Moment
All have been waiting for
Has finally Come!
The Sun is Rising,
Ever so slowly,
Over the Horizon,
And Rise it does,
As it spreads its
Morning Light
Into the hearts
Of all who listen
To that still,
Small voice
Within their hearts.
Nothing can stand
In its Way
Nothing can prevent
Its Coming,
Not now,
Or ever,
Down through
The Corridors of Time,
For this Innocent Child
IS WHO HE IS,
The Word of God
Made Flesh,
Himself in the
Frail, Helpless,
Vulnerable Life
Of an Infant Child—
Praise be the Birth,

That once and only Birth,
That unimaginable Birth,
That ever and forever Birth,
That unique, Incarnate Birth
Of Our Lord, Jesus Christ!

To Our Hearts

Whoever you are,
Whatever your race,
Color,
Nation,
Religion,
Creed,
Or mindset,
I am connected to you
And you to me.
To understand
What this means,
You and I
Need to
Spend some time
In quiet
And allow
The Silence
Within us
To speak
To our hearts.

Together

I walked a path of my own making,
And hoped it would lead me Home.
As I traveled, I began to sense
That the road I had been walking
Had been tread by Someone before.
"Who could this be?" I asked myself.
Who could know beforehand
The path I had carved in Life.
I sat in the quiet of my heart
And listened to what it said.
Then, a quiet voice came and whispered:
"It is I, your Lord and God, who
Has shown you the way Home
All along, from when you first
Came into being,
Until your Journey's End.
Do not be afraid. I love you.
Welcome Me into your heart
And let us travel together."

What I See

With each new day,
I open my eyes.
At the end
Of each day,
I close them.
I spend my nights
In sleep,
Sometimes dreaming,
Sometimes not.
I open my eyes
At the start
Of each new day,
And am comforted
By my belief,
That Someone
Born so long,
Long ago,
Has opened his eyes,
Day after day,
To what I see.

With Gratitude

I take Life
One second,
One minute,
One hour,
One day,
One week,
One month,
One year,
At a time.
Doing so
Allows me
To live Life
In the present
Moment.
Doing so
Allows me
To look
Back on my Life
With Reverence,
Respect,
And Gratitude.

With His

As my memory fades,
Past events disappear
And present happenings
Seem disconnected.
We take so much
For granted in Life,
Being alive,
Air to breathe,
Food to eat,
Education and work,
Family and friends,
Community,
Life and Death,
But the Lord, Our God
Does not take us for granted.
He loves us
In all these things
And promises
To merge our memories
With His.
As my memory fades,
Past events disappear
And present happenings
Seem disconnected.
We take so much
For granted in Life,
Being alive,
Air to breathe,
Food to eat,
Education and work,
Family and friends,
Life and Death,
Community.
But the Lord,
Our God,
Does not take us
For granted.
He loves us
In all these things
And promises,
One day,
To merge
Our memories
With His.

Your Answer?

You live,
And you die.
How
Do
You react
To this?
Either
You believe
In a Life
To Come,
Or You
Do not.
What is
Your answer?

www.ingramcontent.com/pod-product-compliance
Lightning Source LLC
Chambersburg PA
CBHW060849050426
42453CB00008B/915